T0065287

THE FLAMING
TRUTH

INSPIRED BY THE HOLY SPIRIT

ANGELINO A. COOPER

WESTBOW
PRESS®
A DIVISION OF THOMAS NELSON
& ZONDERVAN

WestBow Press books may be ordered through booksellers or by contacting:

WestBow Press
A Division of Thomas Nelson & Zondervan
1663 Liberty Drive
Bloomington, IN 47403
www.westbowpress.com
1 (866) 928-1240

ISBN: 978-1-5127-2700-5 (sc)
ISBN: 978-1-5127-2701-2 (e)

Library of Congress Control Number: 2016900405

Print information available on the last page.

WestBow Press rev. date: 01/28/2016

CONTENTS

This book is dedicated to my grandparents, the late Oscar N. and Sylvia E. Johnson. My grandfather always believed in pursuing the truth, no matter the cost. My grandmother always believed in exhibiting Christ's never-ending love. These two pillars of strength, along with the rest of my family, have encouraged me to seek the truth and to hold firm to my faith in the Lord.

INTRODUCTION

This book was inspired by the Holy Spirit. I was awakened by the Lord at around four in the morning and was moved to write about one topic. I soon discovered that I wanted to share my thoughts on many subjects. Most of these subjects are not new, but they must be addressed. We can no longer keep turning a blind eye to them or sweeping them under the rug. At the end of the day, these issues will remain with us. The Bible is the Word of God, so let's treat it that way and respect what it says. Too many believers are not studying the Word of God but the foolish words of man. I trust that this book will intrigue you and that the Holy Spirit will lead you.

CHAPTER 1

CAST YOUR CARES UPON HIM

Casting all your anxiety onto Him, for He cares for you.

—1 Peter 5:7 NIV

We all have cares, anxieties, and burdens. However, we need not bear them ourselves and become worn down, sick, and discouraged. Jesus, thankfully, gives us a way out. He tells us to turn over every concern to Him. No problem is too small or too great for the Lord. No situation is hopeless. As human beings, we think in the natural world and forget to think in the spirit realm. We believe we can take on the small anxieties and give God the big ones, but we are deceiving ourselves. If we carry any burdens with us, we have a serious dilemma.

We make life more challenging than it has to be. We don't want Jesus to help us with everything, because we want to be independent of Him, so we intentionally hang on to our burdens. Our fleshly natures are predisposed to selfishness and pursue self-glory.

We should never feel saddened about life's circumstances. We have no control over our circumstances, but we can control how we respond to them. The Holy Spirit should always be our guide. He can show us how to overcome our difficulties, but too often we second-guess Him and end up prolonging these problems. We must always speak life into situations and know the power we have over dilemmas.

> Death and life are in the power of the tongue, and those who love it shall eat of the fruit of it. (Proverbs 18:21 NIV)

We cannot do God's work if we are burdened, because we will need as much help as those we want to assist. We must be burden-free believers. Jesus won't force us to relinquish our cares, because He gave us free will. So let's do what we are at liberty to do and give them to the Lord. We must stop believing that we are the ultimate source of knowledge and instead start doing what we need to do. A Christian who knows what to do and does it is a wise person. This is what the world needs: wise people doing the

Lord's work. We must not perish because of a lack of knowledge. I pray all of us will be wise and make use of the knowledge God has given us through His Word. Let us live His Word. After all, He has told us that it is possible to do.

> For my yoke is easy and my burden is light. (Matthew 11:30 NIV)

Let us please Jesus today. Amen.

**Too many burdens
will make you a
nonproductive Christian.**

CHAPTER 2

GOD DOES NOT TOLERATE SEXUAL SIN

> Righteousness lifts up a nation, but sin is a shame to any people. The king's favor is toward a wise servant, but his wrath is against him who causes shame.
>
> —Proverbs 14:34–35 NIV

God knows that this is a perverted generation, but just because He knows this does not mean He accepts it (Acts 2:40). Why are so many people who profess to be Christians caught up in this darkness? I call it darkness because there is no light in these practices. If you are confused about what is darkness and what is light, you need a reality check.

We are out of God's will when we engage in sexual sins. This means He is not with us while we commit these transgressions.

> This is the verdict: Light has come into the world, but men loved darkness instead of light because their deeds were evil. Everyone who does evil hates the light, and will not come into the light for fear that his deeds will be exposed. (John 3:19–20 NIV)

> Likewise every good tree bears good fruit, but a bad tree bears bad fruit. A good tree cannot bear bad fruit, and a bad tree cannot bear good fruit. Every tree that does not bear good fruit is cut down and thrown into the fire. Thus, by their fruit you will recognize them. (Matthew 7:17–20 NIV)

Let's stop looking at the tree and start examining its fruit. We must stop listening to the eloquent words that come out of a person's mouth and start paying attention to the individual's heart.

> You brood of vipers, how can you who are evil say anything good? For out of the overflow of the heart, the mouth speaks. The good man brings good things out of the good stored up in him, and the evil man brings evil things out of the evil stored up in him. (Matthew 12:34–35 NIV)

If you indulge in illicit sexual acts, you're not in good standing with God. You have deliberately left the faith. Your rank or position in a church does not matter. You can be an apostle, a deacon, an elder, a bishop, a pastor, or a teacher, but you are not excluded from sin.

God does not understand a life of habitual sin. If you're shacking up with someone, stop it now! The circumstances do not matter. Because of His holiness, God cannot tolerate sin. Clearly, sin brings spiritual death. Many church leaders habitually sin, committing abominable acts. They have chosen a lifestyle that displeases God. They deceive many and are responsible for compromising the faith of fellow Christians. The result will be catastrophic, with many souls ending up in a godless eternity.

If your pastor is a practicing homosexual, he is not going to heaven. You are wrong if you believe that he knows what he is doing or that because he preaches and prays so well, his lifestyle must be all right with God. You may think he must be on his way to heaven, which means you too are on your way, especially if you come to church faithfully, play a prominent role, and shout yourself hoarse with false worship. You may think that God will sanctify homosexuality because of such ritual observances. Your pastor, who represents God on earth, will tell you that you are correct, but you will wind up where your leader goes if you follow this path.

Both of you, along with everyone else participating in such abominable acts, will end up in hell!

We know God destroyed Sodom and Gomorrah. Let's consider this judgment. God destroyed everyone except for Lot's family. What happened to the teenagers, children, and babies? God destroyed them all because He knew they would live as their parents and leaders lived. If He destroyed precious children who did not know right from wrong, what about those who do? There is no excuse for you. You must stop ignoring the Scripture passages that apply to your sin, because the Bible is God's Word, and it is true. If the Word says an act is sinful, it is, and no sin can enter the kingdom of God.

> Do you not know that the unrighteous shall not inherit the kingdom of God? Do not be deceived; neither fornicators, nor idolaters, nor adulterers, nor abusers, nor homosexuals, nor thieves, nor covetous, nor drunkards, nor revilers, nor extortioners, shall inherit the kingdom of God. (1 Corinthians 6:9–10 NIV)

God will not tolerate a double life, because He wants all of your being. If you desire to enter the kingdom of God, change your life now. Step out of darkness into His marvelous light. There is a way out of darkness, and God is waiting for you to come to the realization of His Word. Be the good tree, bearing good fruit. Let Christ be your mark, and follow all of His commands. Remember that God loved the world so much that He sent Jesus to die for our sins. Jesus has risen and has the power to save us from all sin. God loves all of us.

God is love. Amen.

Don't let your desire drive God away from you.

CHAPTER 3

GOD INHABITS THE PRAISES OF HIS PEOPLE

But thou art holy, O thou that inhabitest the praises of Israel.

—Psalm 22:3 KJV

God indeed inhabits the praises of His people. By meditating on this portion of Scripture, we acquire the faith needed to praise Him. The Lord loves praise, worship, and admiration for being the true and living God.

We benefit from praising God, since praise releases power. Wherever God is, there is power. No darkness can hide in God, because He is pure light (1 John 1:5). Pure light reveals His pure power. We must let God inhabit us, His people. This power should motivate those of us who desire to praise God.

Because of pure darkness, our hearts are hardened and cold toward God. We must break through the darkness into which we were born. We have nothing to do with where we were born or with our birth into sin, but our personal circumstances are not an excuse to stay in this sinful condition.

> When He came near the place where the road goes down the Mount of Olives, the whole crowd of disciples began joyfully to praise God in a loud voice for all of the miracles they had seen: "Blessed is the king who comes in the name of the Lord!' 'Peace in heaven and glory in the highest!" Some of the Pharisees in the crowd said to Jesus, "Teacher, rebuke your disciples!"
> "I tell you," He replied, "if they keep quiet the stones will cry out." (Luke 19:37–40 NIV)

We must not let the rocks cry out to God in our place. He has created us to cry out to Him. He has given us a mind, a tongue, and a mouth to worship Him. I believe that if the rocks and the rest of creation were given the opportunity that God has afforded to us, they would put us to shame. Their cries of praise would be sincere, pure, and unceasing. With our insincere, inconstant, and halfhearted praise, we would not even be close to the rest of creation, which was not made to worship on the earth.

Let us do what we were created to do. We were made in God's image and likeness. We must stop rebelling against our Creator. We must stop ignoring Jehovah and submit. Let us connect to the power that comes through praise. Power comes through praise. We owe the Father this kind of worship.

> Yet a time is coming and now has come when the true worshipers will worship the Father in spirit and truth, for they are the kind of worshipers the Father seeks. God is spirit, and His worshipers must worship in spirit and in truth. (John 4:23–24 NIV)

If we shout hallelujah in our spirits, the word has no other choice but to come through our lips. Let us become true worshippers. Amen.

Praising God is a requirement, not a preference.

CHAPTER 4

LOVE WHAT I LOVE AND HATE WHAT I HATE

And I said, Hear, I pray you, O heads of Jacob, and ye princes of the house of Israel; is it not for you to know judgment? Who hate the good, and love the evil; who pluck off their skin from off them, loves.

—Micah 3:1–2 KJV

We say that we want the mind of Christ, but do we understand His mind? Are we asking for something just for the sake of asking? We say that we are completely committed to Christ Jesus and that we are no longer in control of our lives. We always want more of Him, but we are not using the portion already given to us.

If a glass is full of water, how can we ask for more? To receive fresh water, we must have an empty glass.

We have to live the life of a true Christian, which means acting as Christ did. We must love what He loves and hate what He hates.

Jesus loves the world but hates the sin of the world. However, we in the body of Christ now love evil and hate righteousness. We no longer offer the love of God to others but rather show wickedness to them. Jesus commanded us to love one another, but we do the opposite and hate one another.

> These things I command you, that ye love one another. If the world hate you, ye know that it hated me before it hated you. If ye were of the world, the world would love his own: but because ye are not of the world, but I have chosen you out of the world, therefore the world hateth you. Remember the word that I said unto you, The servant is not greater than his lord. If they have persecuted me, they will also persecute you; if they have kept my saying, they will keep yours also. (John 15:17–20 KJV)

We are putting God's grace to the test. Let us stop abusing the grace He has given us (Romans 6:10). The worst part of this situation is that we think behaving this way is acceptable. It is not! Why is this happening in today's church? The reason is our self-centeredness.

We compromise our standards, which allows us to start loving evil. We have gone astray and are blinded by our selfish deeds. These deeds cause us to hate what is good and to hate the righteous.

We are to fear the Lord and no one else (Matthew 10:28). If we keep our reverence for Yahweh, we will not even consider opposing Him. We will not compromise our standards, as we are now doing. We must remain in the perfect will of God. This will allow us to live as He intends while doing His work. However, doing God's will is not enough. We must not only do His work but live His work. We must strive to live perfected, righteous, God-fearing lives. Any other kind of life is sinful, and if we die in this state, we will hear the Lord say, "Depart from me. I never knew you, worker of iniquity."

> And Jehoshaphat said, Is there not a prophet of the Lord besides, that we might inquire of him? And the king of Israel said unto Jehoshaphat, There is yet one man, Micaiah son of Imlah, by whom we may inquire of the Lord: but I hate him; for he doth not prophesy good concerning me, but evil. And Jehoshaphat said, Let not the king say so. (1 Kings 22:7–8 KJV)

Micaiah did not compromise his message from God just to please the kings, the servants, or the other prophets. He loved the Lord Jehovah too much to do so. We are to be likewise, loving only righteousness and living in a way that reflects this commitment. We must have a personal relationship with God that no one can separate. This close relationship will always keep us in the ways of the Lord.

We were not put on earth for selfish gain. It is so sad to see that the majority of church leaders lead only to obtain wealth. Everything else is secondary, even God. If He is secondary to them, His standards are too. Let's remember to store up our treasures in heaven and not on earth.

It is said that king David was a man after God's own heart. Can this be said of you? David loved what the Lord loved and hated what the Lord hated. If you or I don't do the same, then we are enemies of God.

> Evil shall slay the wicked: and they that hate the righteous shall be desolate. (Psalm 34:21 KJV)
> He deviseth mischief upon his bed; he setteth himself in a way that is not good; he abhorreth not evil. (Psalm 36:4 KJV)
> Ye that love the Lord, hate evil: he preserveth the souls of his saints; he delivereth them out of the hand of the wicked. (Psalm 97:10 KJV)

Make sure you are not an enemy of God (James 4:4). I declare myself to be an enemy of the world and an ally of Jehovah. I hope that all believers have this mind-set.

We must love our fellow believers and even our enemies. Jesus told us to love our neighbors as ourselves (Matthew 22:39). We are to bless those who curse us, to do good to those who hate us, and to pray for them (Matthew 5:44). These blessings are the fruits of a sincere believer. We are to love the Lord with all our hearts, souls, minds, and strength (Mark 12:30). These requirements are written for us to follow. Therefore we have no excuse. We cannot say that we did not know God's commands. Instead, we chose to ignore them.

If you are doing this, you are being hypocritical. A hypocrite will not inherit God's kingdom. I urge you to repent of your ways and to get back into the perfect will of God. None of us is perfect in strength, but we are with the blood of Jesus. God is still in the restoration business. Nothing is impossible for Him. Heaven and earth will pass away, but His word will remain (Mark 13:31). Amen.

The more you love God, the less you will love this world.

CHAPTER 5

MUCH IS REQUIRED

But he that knew not, and did commit things worthy of stripes, shall be beaten with few stripes. For unto whomsoever much is given, of him shall be much required; and to whom men have committed much of him they will ask the more.

—Luke 12:48 KJV

We quote this portion of Scripture all the time but draw the wrong lessons from it. This verse is associated with material blessings, possessions, and wealth, but it is really speaking to spiritual blessings, insights, revelations, and power.

We who are given much do not have a choice. We must share what was given to us. If God has given us knowledge about His kingdom, we have to share this knowledge rather than keep it to ourselves. Knowledge is a gift, and gifts are meant to be shared. Does it make sense for me to keep a present that I have for you? Should I feel comfortable or gratified knowing that I have your gift but that I choose not to give it? This does not make sense. When we receive revelation from God, it is our responsibility to share it, not to hoard it for ourselves, thus becoming self-righteous. It is human nature to want to feel that we're better than others.

In Luke 12:46 KJV Jesus said that "the lord of the servant will come in a day when he does not expect, and at an hour when he does not know. And he will cut him apart, and will appoint him his portion with the unbeliever."

Sons and daughters of the Most High God must not let their portion be with that of the unbelievers. Sad to say, because of their disobedience, too many believers' portions are now with those of the unbelievers. These believers were too lazy to do what God commanded. We have no excuse for failing to share what He has given us; Jesus said that we are required to do this. There is no other option, so why are we not sharing God?

Everything that Jesus did was out of love. He did nothing out of jealousy, selfishness, or envy. He could have no other motive but love because God is love. Love is the reason Jesus Christ was sent to humanity.

God is the greatest person we will ever know. There is none greater than He.

> I give you a new commandment, that you love one another. As I have loved you, you should also love one another. By this all shall know that you are my disciples, if you have love toward one another. (John 13:34–35 NIV)
>
> And now faith, hope and love, these three remain; but the greatest of these is love. (1 Corinthians 13:13 NIV)
>
> For God so loved the world that He gave His only begotten Son that whoever believes in Him should not perish but have everlasting life. (John 3:16 KJV)

It is crystal clear what we are to do, but we turn a blind eye to our obligations. We act lost, as if we do not know our heads from our tails. Some of us actually don't know our heads from our tails. It's the responsibility of those in kingly positions to show others their roles. These kings must help them locate their heads and their tails.

> And Jehovah shall make you the head, and not the tail. And you shall be above and not beneath, if you listen to the commandments of Jehovah your

God, which I command you this day. (Deuteronomy 28:13 NIV)

The head tells the body what to do. If we are the head, we must tell the body of Christ what to do, but Jesus must first be our head. How much of Christ is in us? We all need more of Him. None of us has reached perfection, but we can. We need to stop thinking that this is an unattainable goal.

Holiness is pure, without sin. Let us emulate our Lord, being holy and having no darkness in us.

> For I am Jehovah your God, and you shall sanctify yourselves, and you shall be holy; for I am holy. Neither shall you defile yourselves with any kind of swarming thing that swarms the earth. (Leviticus 11:44 KJV)
>
> Because it is written, "Be holy, for I am holy." (1 Peter 1:16 NIV)

We cannot live in sin or darkness and still think Jesus Christ dwells in us.

> Then Jesus spoke to them again saying, "I am the light of the world. He who follows Me shall not walk in darkness, but shall have the light of life." (John 8:12 NIV)

Let's give ourselves a reality check. We know right from wrong, so let us do what is right and what is required of us. There is no need to run or to hide from it. We have nothing to fear but the Lord.

> And do not fear those who kill body, but rather are not able to kill the soul. But rather fear him who can destroy both soul and body in hell. (Matthew 10:28 NIV)

We must share what we were given to share and do God's will. Too many are lost and are headed for an eternity without Christ. We have got to love them enough to save them from this destruction. Hell is real; otherwise Jesus would not have gone through what He did to save us from it.

Blessed be the name of the Most High God, who lives forevermore.

Hallelujah, hallelujah, hallelujah. Amen.

**Contentment enhances
Jesus's requirement
for believers to
spread the gospel.**

CHAPTER 6

ONCE SAVED IS NOT ALWAYS SAVED

But if a righteous man turns from his righteousness and commits sin and does the same detestable things the wicked man does, will he live? None of his righteous things he has done will be remembered. Because of the unfaithfulness he is guilty of and because of the sins he has committed, he will die.

—Ezekiel 18:24 NIV

This Scripture verse is the subject of much debate. Some say that if people change their lives and live totally for Jesus Christ, they will never turn away from the faith. They will be disciples of Christ, displaying His likeness in their daily lives. I agree with this outlook.

But some people teach a false doctrine, causing controversy. They say that once people have given their lives to Jesus Christ they are saved no matter what they do.

> May they be blotted out the book of life and not be listed with the righteous. (Psalm 69:28 NIV)
>
> He who overcomes will, like them, be dressed in white. I will never blot out his name from the book of life, but will acknowledge his name before my Father and His angels. (Revelation 3:5 KJV)

David, a man after God's own heart, and John, one of Jesus's dearest disciples, both wrote that a person's name can be removed from the Book of Life. This tells us that if someone decides not to live for Christ anymore, his name will be erased. This is quite clear. The apostle Paul also knew this truth.

> Wherefore, my beloved, as ye have always obeyed, not as in my presence only, but now much more in my absence, work out your own salvation with fear and trembling. (Philippians 2:12 KJV)

We cannot even for a day do evil, entertain wicked desires, or indulge the lust of the flesh and believe that we are still on the road to the sweet bye and bye. We need to realize that we have detoured from the upward road to the downward road. The downward road is not the place to be. We cannot make excuses for being on this road to hell. Unfortunately, many people who say they are Christians have left the heavenly road because of their selfishness and don't realize it. We cannot travel on the two roads simultaneously.

> Enter through the narrow gate. For wide is the gate and broad is the road that leads to destruction, and many enter through it. But small is the gate and narrow the road that leads to life, and only a few find it. (Matthew 7:13–14 NIV)

These roads are headed in opposite directions. We must not let ourselves get off track for even a minute. It might turn out to be longer. We must be like our Savior, who never let the Devil have any part of Him. We cannot let the Devil have any part of us. In many cases, the Devil has too much of us and we have too little of Jesus. We must change this situation in order to be triumphant. Jesus wants us to be holy as He is holy. This is possible to do if we imitate Him in thought and in action (1 Peter 1:16). We are to be in His image (Romans 8:29).

> If we confess our sins, He is faithful and just and will forgive us our sins and

purify us from all unrighteousness. (1 John
1:9 NIV)

Let us stop living a lie and start living the truth.
If we sin, God is faithful and just to forgive us of all
our iniquities. But this is not a loophole for us to sin.
Premeditated, habitual sin has consequences. We all
know them, but we act as if we don't. Sexual sins result
in unwanted pregnancy, sexually transmitted diseases,
and even death. For example, a person might be killed
by a jealous lover. This happens much more than we
think. When a person is caught stealing, he may face
incarceration, injury, or death. These are just a few
illustrations of the consequences that may arise even
if we are forgiven by Jesus.

We must know that He wraps Himself in light that
darkness cannot hide (Psalm 139:12). Jesus will forgive
us if we seek His pardon.

"I have fought the good fight, I have finished the
race, I have kept the faith" (2 Timothy 4:7). The race is
not for the swift but for the person who will endure
to the end.

Let us live a true life all the way to the end. Let us
stop believing a lie and live the truth. Amen.

Salvation is a journey of a lifetime, not just one time.

CHAPTER 7

SEXUAL SIN/IMMORALITY CANNOT BE SANCTIFIED

Now the works of the flesh are clearly revealed, which are adultery, fornication, uncleanness and lustfulness.

—Galatians 5:19 KJV

Sexual immorality is widespread in the world today whereas sanctification is seldom practiced. Sexual sin is not sanctified because of a person's title or position in the church.

Let us start at the top positions in the church and work our way down the pyramid. Apostles, preachers, teachers, and evangelists cannot sanctify their sin. They can make excuses for it, downplay it, or turn a blind eye to it, but at the end of the day, they are still in sin. Some believe that the higher up they go in the church, the more they can get away with. The habitual practice of sin dulls their consciences, and they act the same way as all sinners do, lying, stealing, gambling, and hating. The same holds for lay members of the church who kiss up to those in high positions, trying to please man instead of God.

We read God's Word but it does not enter our spiritual hearts, which is where it needs to be. We let everyone else's words take precedence. Everything starts in our hearts. Sin begins in our hearts because all of our innermost desires are rooted there. Jesus said that out of the abundance of the heart the mouth speaks. That is why it is important to listen to what comes out of a person's mouth (Matthew 12:34). The heart of man is filthy, and sin originates there. Jesus said that a person committing adultery in the heart has sinned (Matthew 5:28). We ask, "How can I sin just by thinking about something?" When we surrender to our deep desires and emotions, we commit sinful acts in our heads.

All of us have fallen short of God's glory and should be encouraged to get back on track.

> David says, "I have hidden Your Word in my heart, so that I might not sin against You" (Psalm 119:11).

We need to hide God's Word in our hearts. When we hide something, it is hard for others to find it. Only we can locate it at will. We cannot keep the Word of God skin deep. Too many sincere believers do this, and their weakness is exposed during times of testing and trial. This is why they give in to immoral temptations. We need to keep the Word deep in our hearts and the immorality skin deep. Then we will not fall or desire to yield to temptation, because the awesome love we have for God deep within will overwhelm foolish superficial thoughts of perversion.

When we look back at our sexual immorality, we will wonder how it could have made any sense at all, and we will thank God for saving us from guilt and shame. Sin is shameful; it allows the Enemy of God to control our minds. Even when we repent, we are continually beating ourselves over the head. We must not be preoccupied with this self-pity, which is a sin, since there is too much work to be done for the kingdom. We have souls to win for Christ, the only one who can sanctify our sins.

> And they shall keep my ordinance, lest they bear sin for it, that they may not die for it when they defile it. I, Jehovah, sanctify them. (Leviticus 22:9 NIV)

We should not assume that God will overlook sexual immorality because of a person's works. We should not waste time contemplating the technicalities surrounding a sin. Either it is sin or it is not. The apostle

Paul states clearly that persons who practice such things shall not inherit the kingdom of God. Notice that he says "shall not" rather than "might not." This means there is no room for debate.

> Now the works of the flesh are manifest, which are these; adultery, fornication, uncleanness, lasciviousness, idolatry, witchcraft, hatred, variance, emulations, wrath, strife, seditions, heresies, envying, murders, drunkenness, revellings, and such like: of which I tell you and told you before, as I have also told you in time past, that they which do such things shall not inherit the kingdom of God. (Galatians 5:19–21 KJV)

Jesus tells us that many will say, "Look at all the works I have done!" What we have done for Jesus counts only if it is the will of God, not our will. Let us not be among the many!

> Many will say to me in that day, Lord, Lord, have we not prophesied in thy name? And in thy name cast out devils? And in thy name done many wonderful works? And then will I profess unto them, I never knew you: depart from me, ye that work iniquity. (Matthew 7:22–23 KJV)

Let us compare our judgment of what is right and wrong with God's judgment of what is right and wrong and conform accordingly. We must follow those who follow Jesus Christ, not just in words but in deeds. Too many of us confine our faith to words and are not godly. The Scriptures have spoken; God has spoken. No sin can be sanctified except through Jesus Christ, who is the Lamb of God. Jesus is always ready to forgive us, but He says we must stop sinning.

Let us live this Word. Hallelujah. Amen.

**Perpetual sinning is
not repented sin.**

CHAPTER 8

THE TRUTH WILL SET YOU FREE

And you shall know the truth, and the truth shall make you free. They answered Him, we are Abraham's seed and were never in bondage to anyone. How do you say, you will be made free? Jesus answered them, truly, truly, I say to you, whoever practices sin is the slave of sin. And the slave does not abide in the house forever, but the Son abides forever. Therefore if the Son shall make you free, you shall be free indeed.

—John 8:32–36 NIV

Telling the truth is a hard thing to do. The truth will set us free, but it comes with consequences. The world, however, still respects people who tell the truth and is somewhat lenient in punishing them. Jesus wants us to be free from sin, but this does not necessarily mean physical freedom. We want physical freedom, but we will not always get it for telling the truth. However, it is far better in the long run to be free from sin than to be freed by a lie and to be a slave to sin.

Many people choose natural freedom over spiritual freedom. Jesus tells us that the natural body will not last forever but that the spirit is eternal. If we put things in the proper perspective, we will have no difficulty in making the correct decision. The practice of truth telling will develop the character of Christ in us. This will drive us to keep God's Word in our hearts. If we do not violate God's law, we will not be placed in difficult situations and have to lie to escape them.

Some people do what is right in the sight of God, but because they fear rejection, they lie to fit in. They want to serve God in secret but publicly are ashamed of Him. Jesus says that if we are ashamed of Him, He will be ashamed of us.

> But whoever shall deny Me before men, I will also deny him before My Father in heaven. (Matthew 10:33 KJV)

We should not worry about being rejected by men but about being rejected by God.

The book of Romans explains the benefits of telling the truth: "But now, being made free from sin, and having become slaves to God, you have your fruit to holiness, and the end everlasting life" (Romans 6:22 NIV).

We will always be slaves, but we must decide whose slave we want to be: a slave of the Devil or a slave of Christ. "For when you were the slaves of sin, you were free from righteousness" (Romans 6:20 NIV).

If we have not decided to live for Christ, we have decided to keep living in sin. We stay in it because it is so sweet and then remain slaves to the Devil. We don't feel compelled to do what is right, because we were born sinful and thus do not have righteousness in us.

Jesus Christ is sweeter than the sweetest sin, so we should have no problem being slaves to Him. We can live in righteousness through Jesus Christ, our Savior.

The truth will set us eternally free, allowing us to become holy and righteous and to gain everlasting life. However, we must remain voluntary slaves to Jesus Christ. Let us keep these Scripture passages in our hearts. This will help us in seemingly difficult circumstances. Eternal freedom should be our goal.

Give glory to God in the highest. Amen.

Spiritual freedom is better than physical freedom.

CHAPTER 9

WORSHIP HIM IN SPIRIT AND TRUTH, NOT IN SPIRIT AND A LIE

But the hour is coming, and now is, when the true worshipers shall worship the Father in spirit and truth, for the Father seeks such to worship Him. God is a spirit, and they who worship Him must worship in spirit and truth.

—John 4:23–24 KJV

What is Jesus talking about when He says that worship must be done in the spirit but also in the truth? He is showing us how we must worship. God is a spirit, and we are also spirit beings, living in the physical housing of our bodies. This is why we live forever even when our bodies die. We are in these bodies for an allotted time, and during this time, we should worship our

Creator wholeheartedly. We were created in His image for this purpose.

> And God created man in His image; in the image of God created he him; male and female created he them. (Genesis 1:27 KJV)

Anyone who chooses not to worship God will be separated from Him forever. This eternal separation, known as hell, was not designed for us but is a reality for those who remain wicked. We put our souls on the line daily if we delay choosing Jesus Christ, our precious Redeemer.

> The Spirit Himself bears witness with our spirit that we are the children of God. (Romans 8:16 KJV)

Our spirit communicates with the Holy Spirit, who is God. To worship God in spirit, we must have His Spirit in us. But to do this, we must first be saved, accepting Jesus Christ, the Lamb of God, into our hearts.

Before we are saved, we have a void in us, and only Jesus Christ can fill it. When we are saved, this void is filled by the Holy Spirit, who now dwells in us. It is impossible for us to worship God in spirit if His Spirit is not in us. Without His Spirit, we will have no connection to God, and without a connection, there can be no communication. This is the reason many unsaved people do not waste their time pretending to worship God. However, many people will pretend to worship God to receive recognition, to appear holy, and to spread false doctrine. All of these aims are detestable wickedness from the pit of hell.

> Likewise the Spirit also helpeth our infirmities: for we know not what we should pray for as we ought: but the Spirit itself maketh intercession for us with groaning which cannot be uttered. (Romans 8:26 KJV)

The Holy Spirit is our direct line to God. Most of the time our spirit does not know what to ask for, and so the Holy Spirit will step in and guide us in our talks with God. The Spirit often prompts us on how and when to worship and tells us why we need to worship. True worship brings forth the power from on high, and unimaginable events occur.

> I will also praise thee with the psaltery, even thy truth, O my God: unto thee will I sing with the harp, O thou Holy One of Israel. (Psalm 71:22 KJV)

We must proclaim the truth about God to Him. King David was an expert at praising God for His faithfulness, graciousness, mercy, and truth. We must lift up God's holy name, proclaim His never-ending love for us, and declare His righteousness in songs. This pleases God. We should never cease to say how grateful we are to Him for sending His only Son to redeem humanity.

> God forbid: yea, let God be true, and every man a liar; as it is written, that thou mightest be justified in thy sayings, and mightest overcome when thou art judged. (Romans 3:4 KJV)

Everything about God is true. His Word is life, and we must believe what we say when we declare His Word. We must live lives of worship, and true worship is found in obedience. We cannot live a lie and declare with our mouths the truths about God. That would make us hypocrites. We have too many hypocrites in the house of God, and they are leading people astray. These hypocrites are of the Satan, and we know his agenda: to destroy lives. God does not tolerate hypocrisy, because this is a type of darkness. There is no darkness in God. He is pure, holy, and sweet, radiating light. We are to be of like mind and to stand against darkness, not just some but all manner of evil.

Anyone who does not worship or serve God in spirit and in truth will be destroyed on the day of judgment. Our circumstances will not matter; our hardships will not matter; the neglect or abuse we suffered will not matter. God will not accept these excuses and admit us into His kingdom. We can enter through only one door, and that door is Jesus Christ.

> The Son of man shall send forth his angels, and they shall gather out of his kingdom all things that offend, and them which do iniquity; and shall cast them into a furnace of fire: there shall be wailing and gnashing of teeth. (Matthew 13:41–42 KJV)

It is impossible for us to deceive God. Let's stop offending Him and stop pretending to Him. Let us love and serve God with our whole hearts; this is what He wants from us. God is tired of false worshippers who know that they are living a lie and are behaving contrary to Him. Our fellow men cannot save us, so if we are trying to impress or to fool them, how does this benefit us? It is not profitable, and all those living a lie must repent now before it's too late.

We must stop living defeated lives and tap into the divine power through true worship. This worship brings deliverance out of every situation. We must allow ourselves to be delivered from our sinful, repulsive nature. No matter how morally we live, there is no good in any of us. We must make a conscious effort to seek Jesus with all of our might. God is looking about the earth for true worshippers. Let Him find us ready.

A life of truth will reveal the glory of God, and a life of deception will reveal the face of Satan. There are only two sides; we must choose whom we want to reveal. If we have chosen God's glory, we must let it shine out of us. Playtime has been over for a long time. It is now wartime! Let us be free from sin. True worship will bring out the Son of God in us. He is inside each of us who profess His name, but He will not force Himself out of us. We must bring out the God in us, and this will happen only with a lifestyle of truth.

For the Lord is a God of truth, the awesome Creator of the world, a holy God. Amen.

Don't be a false worshipper, because that won't profit you.

CHAPTER 10

THE POWER OF PRAYER

The Lord is far from the wicked: but he heareth the prayer of the righteous.

—Proverbs 15:29 KJV

Confess your faults one to another, and pray one for another, that ye may be healed. The effectual fervent prayer of a righteous man availeth much.

—James 5:16 KJV

Wow! What a statement about the power of prayer! There is no greater weapon than prayer for spiritual warfare. Remember that our fight is not against flesh and blood but against spiritual wickedness in high places (Ephesians 6:12).

What is prayer? Is it a lot of eloquent words softly spoken?

Prayer is, in fact, a dialogue with God. It simply means talking to Him. It's up to us if we want to complicate this conversation with a bunch of self-righteous gibberish, or if we want to be sincere and to pour out our hearts to Him. We are given clear instructions on the frequency of our prayers to God. We are told by the apostle Paul to pray without ceasing (1 Thessalonians 5:17).

God wants us to communicate constantly with Him. We are to bring all of our concerns to Him to get His advice, and we are also to receive instructions on the work that we need to do. We cannot rely on ourselves to do things for God, because we will fall into error and be defeated. We will end up basing our actions on feelings and desires. We cannot operate on emotions. Instead we must be Spirit-led (Romans 8:14). We must no longer rely on self-will but on God's will; we therefore have to die to self. We should note that Jesus Christ, the Son of the Most High God, did not do His own will but rather the will of His Father in heaven. So what gives us the right to think that we can do otherwise? Jesus said that the servant is not greater than the master, so let us stop mixing things up and acting according to our own wills.

Jesus has given us the Lord's Prayer as an example of how we are to pray, or to talk with God. His example is, of course, a perfect one because He was the perfect man on earth and is the perfect God who reigns forevermore. Hallelujah! In His example of talking with God, Jesus shows us how to reverence the heavenly Father by exalting His name, Yahweh. We are also to ask for God's will to be done. We are to pray daily to God for the strength to do His will and for the daily provisions needed to live while we are on this earth.

The Lord also wants us to be cognizant of the daily trials and temptations we will face. We do not have to give in to these temptations. When confronted with them, we are to immediately ask for help from on high to pass the test set before us. All of our trials are tests intended to take us to the next spiritual level. Many of us are curious about why we remain at the same faith level for years. The answer is simple: we keep failing the test, and to move forward, we must pass it. Aren't you tired of failing the same test over and over again? I sure am.

Some of us develop lackadaisical, defeatist attitudes. We Christians cannot afford to have this lazy mentality. It's a good thing that Jesus did not have these attitudes. Otherwise He would not have been able to accomplish His mission. But He had a secret—the power of prayer. This power was the only thing that kept Him going, enabling Him to fulfill the will of God. If Jesus could do it, so can we. He gave us all of the power that He had on this earth. We can do all things through Christ, who strengthens us to achieve the goal of perfection.

Many great men and women of God have been able to do mighty works and unfathomable things for God.

They had a secret weapon to accomplish these goals, prayer. Talking with God makes everything possible. Nothing is too hard for my God; nothing is impossible. Maybe your god has limitations, but my God does not.

As human beings it is natural for us to think and to behave like the persons we are most often with. We start to emulate certain of their attributes, be they positive or negative. For this reason, Jesus tells us to abide in Him.

> Abide in me, and I in you. As the branch cannot bear fruit of itself, except it abide in the vine; no more can ye, except ye abide in me. I am the vine, ye are the branches: he that abideth in me, and I in him, the same bringeth forth much fruit: for without me you can do nothing. If a man abide not in me, he is cast forth as a branch, and is withered; and men gather them, and cast them into the fire, and they are burned. If ye abide in me, and my words abide in you, ye shall ask what ye will, and it shall be done unto you. (John 15:4–7 KJV)

The Lord's thoughts will become our thoughts, and our thoughts His thoughts. We will want to do only what we dwell on, and that is the perfect will of God. The prophet Elijah had such a relationship with God. This relationship allowed him to pray for the rain to stop "according to my word" (1 Kings 17:1). It is particularly important that this happened under his authority. We might ask how it was possible for a man to use this authority? The reason is that Elijah's will lined up with God's will. Elijah dwelled with God, and this allowed him to think like God.

If we are going to achieve greatness in the kingdom, we must keep company with God. We are to stay in and around Him at all times, never stopping our communication with Him. Then we will know His voice. Jesus says, "My sheep hear my voice" (John 10:27). Too many of us Christians don't hear and know the Almighty's voice. This causes a huge problem for us. We want to do God's work, but we can't hear what work He wants us to do. The result is catastrophic as we find ourselves doing other people's jobs, mistakenly believing that these are our tasks. Everything is out of whack when this happens. We end up working hard but accomplishing nothing for God. This is why we are to know the voice of God and to follow His instructions to the letter. Our time is too short to spend it doing somebody else's job. God has given us special individual skills, and only we can do the tasks that He has assigned us.

Let us do our part and stay in touch with Jesus. He is always available to us, though we do not always make ourselves available to Him. We choose to pick up the receiver or to hang up when it's convenient for us. Let's stop stretching the grace that God so richly bestows upon us. We must get our priorities in the right order by putting God first and everything else next. I'll make an effort to do so; I hope you'll do the same.

If nothing else changes things, praying or talking to God sure does. Amen.

Time spent in prayer brings success in our lives.

CONCLUSION

I trust that this book has ministered to you. I hope you were enlightened and will never be the same. The church has too many talkers and not enough walkers. You may be asking the Lord, "Where are all of the real disciples?" The answer is quite simple. Start with yourself. Become what God is looking for in a disciple of Christ. Always be led by the Spirit, and God will do the rest. He loves all of us abundantly, so don't let Him down.